For Nina, Laurance, and John,
Pirate spirits to be.
love,
Steve
10/21/82

Are You Pirates?

by Steven Kroll

Pictures by Marylin Hafner

PANTHEON BOOKS NEW YORK

Library of Congress Cataloging in Publication Data
Kroll, Steven. Are you pirates? Summary: A carpenter's apprentice who yearns to be a pirate finally gets the experience and finds out
it's nothing like he'd imagined.   [1. Pirates—Fiction]   I. Hafner, Marylin.   II. Title.   PZ7.K9225Ar 1983   [E]   80-27621
ISBN 0-394-83936-6   ISBN 0-394-93936-0 (lib. bdg.)

For Lincoln Anderson
S. K.

For Larry L. and Jennifer C.
—who threw me a rope
M. H.

Tom Burke was a carpenter's apprentice. But all the time he spent in Mr. Collins' shop, he spent daydreaming about pirates.

He wanted to be a scar-faced captain at the helm of a sleek black ship.

He wanted to duel down the deck of a golden Spanish galleon, scattering Spaniards left and right.

He wanted to drink rum with his grizzled mates and run his fingers through piles of gold doubloons.

He was so busy daydreaming, he didn't get much work done.

One noon, with his lunch in hand, Tom went for a walk in the woods. In the middle of a clearing, three strange-looking men were shoveling dirt into a big chest.

Suddenly the tall one with the earring pointed a pistol at Tom. "All right, mates," he said to the others. "Get over here and tie up this lad! He's got the makings of a fine cabin boy."

The two men lunged for Tom. One man fell in the hole. The other fell in the chest.

"Well," said the tall man with the earring, "why don't you just come along anyway?"

"Sure," said Tom. "Are you pirates?"

The tall man smiled. "Of course!" he said.

The pirates marched off to the harbor. On the way, Tom asked, "What were you doing with that chest?"

"Just practicing," said the tall pirate, "for when we get our treasure."

"But you left the chest behind," said Tom.

"Yup," came the reply. "But at least we have another."

They climbed into the jolly boat and pushed off. The boat began to sink.

"Hard Luck Harris!" shouted the tall pirate as the water reached his knees. "You forgot to check for leaks!"

Harris looked upset. The men swam for the ship. Tom swam with them. He wasn't going to miss his chance to be a pirate.

Soon they reached the pirate ship and began climbing the rope ladder.

"Watch your step!" the tall pirate shouted.

Hard Luck Harris stopped and stared at his feet. Everyone else had to stop, too.

"Harris!" shouted the tall pirate. "I didn't mean watch your feet. I meant be careful climbing the ladder. Now hurry up!"

When everyone was finally on deck, the tall pirate introduced Tom to Captain Johnny Red.

The captain shook Tom's hand. "Welcome aboard," he said. "You've met my mate, Mad Mike, here. And you've probably seen enough of Harris. Let's see if I can find the rest of the crew." He cleared his throat. "Juice and sea biscuits!" he yelled.

Everyone lined up on deck.

"Juice, not rum?" Tom asked.

"Gets 'em every time," said the captain. "Now let's see. Here's Fightin' Fred. Cutlass Carl. Awful Arthur. Ghastly Gordon. Scary Scott. Pungent Paul. Lousy Louie. Nasty Nick. Ruthless Robert. Terrible Toby. Toothless Tim. Fearless Frank. Where's Sleepy Sam?"

Suddenly a huge splash rocked the ship.

"What was that?" shouted the captain.

"Beggin' your pardon, sir," said Lousy Louie. "That was Sleepy Sam, sleepwalking again. Bumped right into the cannon, and knocked it overboard."

"Can't Sam ever stay awake? Now we've lost our cannon!" said the captain.

"Well, sir," said Louie, "at least we have another."

Tom hoped the ship had two of everything.

"You, boy," said the captain. "Come with me."

Inside the captain's cabin there was a big sea chest.

"Do you have lots of treasure in there?" Tom asked.

The captain opened the chest. At the bottom was the biggest box of candy Tom had ever seen.

"You can have some," said the captain. "But only after lights out. Now sign the ship's articles with your mark."

Tom looked down at the piece of paper. It said:

RULES and REGULATIONS:

1 No fighting.
2 No stealing.
3 No one gets stuck on a desert island.
4 No one walks the plank.
5 Lights out at 7:30.

"I don't understand," Tom said. "Aren't pirates supposed to fight and steal?"

"Of course," said the captain. "No one follows the rules on this ship."

Tom signed the bottom of the paper with an X, the way pirates always did.

The *Scavenger* headed out to sea. The captain climbed into the rigging with his spyglass.

"Remember the pirates' code," he shouted to the crew. "All ships are fair game. Red ones. Blue ones. Purple ones. But gold ones get three stars!"

"Bingo!" shouted Toothless Tim. "A golden Spanish galleon is on the horizon!"

The crew got ready and the *Scavenger* sneaked up from behind.

"Prepare to board!" shouted Mad Mike.

Five pirates threw out hooks to tie the two ships together. All five pirates went flying into the water.

"Aren't they supposed to let go of their ropes?" asked Tom.

"Of course they are," said the captain. "I've told them a million times."

Just then the *Scavenger* rammed right into the golden Spanish galleon. The *Scavenger*'s crew went flying onto the galleon's deck. Tom landed behind a barrel. Pirates were dashing everywhere.

Captain Johnny Red came dueling down the deck.

"Wow!" Tom thought. "At last, a real battle!"

"Take that!" the captain said, spearing a hat into the air.

"Gimme back my hat!" the enemy officer yelled.

"I know that voice," said the captain. "And I know that face, too!"

"It's me, you old thief," said the officer. "Your old pal, Benny the Bold."

Just then the *Scavenger* rammed right into the golden Spanish galleon. The *Scavenger*'s crew went flying onto the galleon's deck. Tom landed behind a barrel. Pirates were dashing everywhere.

Captain Johnny Red came dueling down the deck.

"Wow!" Tom thought. "At last, a real battle!"

"Take that!" the captain said, spearing a hat into the air.

"Gimme back my hat!" the enemy officer yelled.

"I know that voice," said the captain. "And I know that face, too!"

"It's me, you old thief," said the officer. "Your old pal, Benny the Bold."

"Benny the Bold of the *Jolly Robber*?"

"Same one."

"This isn't a golden Spanish galleon?"

"Nah. We're pirates, like always. We're in disguise."

"So the battle is over?"

"Yeah. How about some ice cream?"

"Ice cream?"

"Yeah. We just robbed the good ship *Humor*. Got every flavor. Chocolate chip. Vanilla. Coconut. Come and get it."

The pirates cheered and hurried to the *Jolly Robber*'s galley. Ice cream bars flew everywhere.

Tom had a coconut bar and a butterscotch sundae. Then he joined the *Scavenger*'s crew in their favorite song:

YO HO
Here we Go,
SAILING HIGH
AND SAILING LOW.
YO HO, we're so bold
Give us all YOUR GOLD.
YO HO it's JUST OUR DISH,
AN ICE CREAM BAR
AND A KETTLE OF FISH.
YO HO We're so BOLD,
Give us all YOUR GOLD!

THIS SIDE UP

He wondered if all pirate battles ended with ice cream.

After the party, nobody on the *Scavenger* felt like having supper. Tom went to bed early, wondering if Mr. Collins missed him at the shop. Around midnight, he woke up hungry.

"The captain's candy," he thought.

He crept down the deck and opened the door to the captain's cabin.

He stepped inside and crashed right into Hard Luck Harris.

"What's going on here?" the captain shouted.

"Come for some candy, sir," said Tom from the floor.

"Nonsense," said the captain. "No one has any candy except after lights out."

"But it is after lights out."

"It's not *after* lights out," said the captain. "The lights *are* out. You saw the rules and regulations."

"But you said no one follows the rules on this ship," said Tom.

"That's right!" said the captain. "And that's why you're going to a desert island, Harris. And Tom Burke, you're going to walk the plank. I've had enough."

Tom was beginning to wish he'd never heard of pirates.

Tom and Harris spent the rest of the night under heavy guard. In the morning, the captain led Tom to the plank.

"Bring the blindfold!" he ordered.

Nasty Nick stepped forward and blindfolded the captain.

Johnny Red waved his cutlass. "Off you go, Tom Burke!" he shouted.

The crew hissed and booed.

The plank was springy, like a diving board. Tom jumped down hard on the end and soared into the rigging. From his perch he scanned the horizon.

"Land ho!" he shouted.
"There's our desert island," said the captain.

Hard Luck Harris was dumped on the island.

"Good-bye and good luck!" everyone yelled as the *Scavenger* began to sail away.

Harris ran along the shore after it. He fell into a large hole.
   Looking back at the island, Tom saw Harris throwing coins and jewels into the air.

"Captain," he said, "I think we should go back. Harris found a treasure."

"Nonsense," said the captain, looking out to sea. "Hard Luck Harris couldn't find a treasure if he fell on it."

That night a storm came up. The *Scavenger* was thrown off course. The ship pitched and moaned. The winds howled. The rigging shook. Tom and the crew hung on to the rail.

"Strike the mainsail!" shouted the captain.

"Heave ho!" shouted Mad Mike.

And down came the sail.

"Get me out of here," cried the captain, tossing and kicking under the canvas. "This is the last straw!"

By now Tom was feeling the same way.

In the morning, the storm was over and the sea was calm again. The *Scavenger* was back in harbor. So was the *Jolly Robber*. Benny the Bold and his crew and Hard Luck Harris were busy unloading a chest filled with gold and jewels.

"Hey, Captain," yelled Mad Mike. "Benny the Bold rescued Hard Luck Harris!"

"Yeah," yelled Nasty Nick. "And they're all going to be rich!"

There was a big splash off the stern of the ship. The captain rowed by in the jolly boat.

"There goes the captain," shouted the crew.

"Well," said Lousy Louie, "don't we have another?"

Mad Mike turned to Tom. "Are you interested?" he asked.

"Are you kidding?" Tom said. "I'd rather be a carpenter."

Mad Mike ducked as a pirate fell from the crosstrees. "Well, all right," he said. "I'll take you ashore."

When he was safe on shore, Tom watched Mad Mike get halfway to the ship, begin to sink, and start swimming. A little boy was watching, too.

"Are you pirates?" he asked.

"No such thing," said Tom.

STEVEN KROLL grew up in New York City and graduated from Harvard University. He has been an editor both here and in England, and has been a full-time writer since 1969. His short stories and reviews have appeared in many leading magazines and newspapers, and he has written over a dozen books for children. He lives in Manhattan.

MARYLIN HAFNER was born in Brooklyn, New York, and studied art at Pratt Institute and the School of Visual Arts. She has illustrated more than thirty-five books for children, and is also a sculptor and printmaker. She has three grown daughters and now lives in Cambridge, Massachusetts.